Hollywood comes to the Rez:

Images in Transformation

Native Americans and the evolution of Indian Film Icons

Lori J. Taguma

"Three things will last forever - faith, hope and love. The greatest of these is love."

I Corinthians 13:13.

CONTENTS

Foreword: From the LCO Reservation, 2019.

Back in the 1990's when a new generation of Native Americans found renewed potential through academics, artists wrote about their experiences from inside reservation boundaries and culture, shining a light on aspects of Native America in a way that has continued to influence American culture. Native Americans, as do writers from other marginalized cultures or classes, write for our lives, while shining a light on injustice and reality. Telling our stories, for better or worse, is a transformational and profound experience. Since returning to the northern Wisconsin reservation where I was raised in 2006, I have found that it is the light of God, shining through our faith community and rooted in the word of God, that has sustained me throughout my journey.

I am immensely thankful to the people who have helped me throughout my life, who have led and accompanied me on transformative journeys, some for brief moments, and some walking closely with me. These journeys include the spiritual, physical, and academic, in locations ranging from the north woods of Wisconsin, to Hawaii, Kansas, Utah, Arizona, and Mexico, to the Pacific Ocean and back. My family and friends, on reservation and off, mean so much to me. Fellow students, board members, mentors, professors, artists, attorneys, sailors and windsurfers, scientists, anthropologists, native cousins, doctors, nurses, pastors, administrators, survivors, and my dearest sisters and brothers in faith.

We are all in transformation, some on the fringe, some in the midst of it all, some with one foot in each world. We who have walked together have become family. I have seen and experienced great change occurring at the intersections of faith and grace, for myself and others. I have learned that through it all, we are enlightened by the guidance of our heavenly father. Our contact shapes our experiences, yet everything is meant for his glory. I am so thankful for my brothers and sisters in Christ, who have accompanied me on this journey. My small group members, and prayer warriors in sanctuaries, theaters, homes, garages, schools, churches, cabins, who have offered many healing transformative prayers, and have shared enlightening experiences and teachings. I am so blessed to know you children of god who are from different cultures, races, societies. We are all from the family of man.

While attending the University of California at Berkeley in the 1990's, my experience as a returning student from Wisconsin via Southern California, was profound. I found an academic haven on the UCB campus which was enriching in many ways. I am thankful to the community who welcomed me, including the American Indian Child Resource Center, AIHC, UIN, the Native Film Institute, AFI, multiple California Jr. Colleges, the UC Berkeley campus Administration and Professors, the Berkeley City and Arts community, Marin Scholarship Foundation, fellow students on campus, the UCB sailing and windsurfing community, and others I may have overlooked. My life at UC Berkeley was continually enriched by the people, countless libraries, cafes, swimming pools, museums and theaters on campus, as well as the expansive Bay Area region, which provided a rich environment for theoretical exploration and personal development. I am forever grateful for the opportunity to connect with amazing individuals, who eagerly shared their knowledge, life experiences, love of their fellow men and women, and extended opportunities for character development and guidance.

The UC Berkeley professors whose courses and office hours I attended, as well as the encounters with professors and graduate student professors on campus, were always engaging, intense, and entertaining. I appreciated the friendships and opportunity to study and engage in educational explorations that were profound and amazing. From the time I entered campus, (Bridgett and Earl) there was no lack of academic and social stimulation, from encountering the naked man who was a student on campus and featured on the cover of Time magazine, to dining at the International House with students and professors representing countries from around the world. Holding Geronimo's war club in the UCB's Phoebe Hearst Museum Archives, while accessing the historical audio and video archives of Native America, as well as the historical archives of every other culture imaginable, was fabulous. I experienced an amazing physical transformation while accompanying UCB Professor Huston Smith and Kifaru Productions, in an exploration of Native American religious freedom, while filming ceremonial preparations in a pre-Colombian Mexican village. Shortly afterwards, I experienced a similarly profound spiritual transformation, while sailing the Bay with some of the nicest people in the world. Creating documentaries in the Anthropology

4

Department with amazing professors, and working with other filmmakers and artists from the American Indian Film Festival and Berkeley City Arts Commission, were also truly enlightening experiences.

Sailing and windsurfing the Bay with some of the heartiest group of people on earth, and now skiing and biking the Birkebeiner trail in northern Wisconsin with hearty, spirited believers, has truly brought me closer to God. Building trust in fellow men and women, with resilience built by wrestling with the larger natural elements of wind, water and snow, has provided a mind body healing for my soul. Mountain biking Mt. Tam, while watching the fog roll in under the Bay Bridge, put God's work in perspective. Sailing, skiing, biking teaches resilience; trust built by setting a point of sail into dense fog, or bouncing off waves and water while strapped onto a surfboard and sail, thoroughly melds mind and body. Similarly, skiing the Wisconsin Birkebeiner trail in the springtime, flying through the trees on skiis or mountain bikes, perfecting technique, surrounded by God's amazing creation, provides restoration for the soul and spirit. Resilience, justice, restoration, redemption. Sports related adrenolin can be transformative for mind and body; being filled with the holy spirit provides ultimate renewal. Thank you to the angels who speak truth and create justice. My time spent on the Art Commission at Berkeley, also provided perfect opportunities to choose artistic voices combining spiritual, reflexive art for public enjoyment.

Through it all, I have felt God's hand over me; he is the glue that has led me, saved me many times, and filled the gaps. He has become closer still, here in northern Wisconsin during prayer meetings in sanctuaries, at home, and in backwoods cabins. He is present and I have become surrounded by his angels who have multiplied. His army is led by his children from all cultures, demographics and areas of life, members of small groups from different churches and places of worship who are healers, teachers, and warriors.

Dr. Kathy Moran led me through the academic thesis process in the UC Berkeley American Studies Department back in the 1990s, where the plethora of amazing professors and administrators were most likely amazed at my lack of knowledge, but valued who I was and where I had come from. I absolutely enjoyed my conversations with them during office hours and beyond, from the first draft of this thesis, December 20, 1996, with Dr. Kathy Moran, through the second draft, edited by Laura Hall in

May 1997, and then a final draft January 10, 1999, edited by Dr. Kathy Moran. I contemplated other versions which included the similarities and parallels of Native American artistic development with Renaissance poetics, while immersed in that time period in one of the many UC Berkeley libraries.

After returning to my home in Northern Wisconsin in 2006, I decided to comment on and publish my University of California Berkeley Bachelor of Arts thesis, which was derived from interview sources and course content, so carefully thought about years ago. The development of native ideals and morality as people, is now more relevant than ever. Native American artists, especially filmmakers, create imagery which is realistic, stylized and at times heart wrenching, showing both the beauty and the underlying darkness in the Native cultural experience. The content speaks to the development of cultures and communities in general, combined with my collective experiences on and off campus and on reservations, while interacting with folks from the Native Film Festival, Sundance Film Festival, LCO and other tribal communities, the Anthropology Department, American Studies, Ethnic Studies, Native American Studies, and Swedish Film Studies Departments, the Berkeley Art Commission, City of Berkeley, American Indian Child Resource Center, AFI, Churches and sanctuaries, and Cal Sailing organization.

I am consistently drawn to creative, spirited people who live with humility, believe in healthy sustainable development, and create beauty in many ways. I have learned through experience how we live by faith in God, from my sisters and brothers in faith who provide a highly developed moral compass, here in a little town in northern Wisconsin, and similarly in a little town in Hawaii, both places where my ancestors have lived by following the word of God for generations. For better or worse, we are tied to one another and face the same issues.

Now I'm living at home on the reservation where I was raised. My ancestors who signed the treaty of La Point in the 1800s, claimed hunting, gathering and fishing rights on these ceded territories where our family members have lived since the inception of the Tribe. During my first year back home in 2006, I felt as if I had stepped into the 1970s. I was told endlessly, "This is how it's always been." Since that time, together with other courageous women and men who stand in the gap for justice, we have fought against the dark social forces that diminish lives, perpetuate violence, and harm family and community. We have fought from inside the reservation and surrounding area, against those who misuse our sovereignty while perpetuating gang and drug violence, and corruption; we fight for effective healthy change. We fight for the abolishment of the lawless gang presence and drug dealers, who sow a "culture of violence," and "take without conscience," systematically here on this reservation and on others, targeting the most vulnerable women, elders and humble tribal members. The cycles of domestic, sexual and systemic abuse, corruption, and apathy have left many people on reservations impoverished and hopeless. We fight against those who have misused the tools that God has given them. We are the resistance, fighting for justice here in our homelands, from within the culture.

Through it all, I have experienced a renewed faith in God's word, and am so blessed by the courageous brothers and sisters who walk beside us. As believers and survivors, we have brought light to lives by speaking our stories through word, print and images, in sanctuaries, churches, courts and schools, and by taking a stand against evil. The reason I am here is to live the life that God has planned for me, to honor and build on the generations of hard work, and accomplishments of my ancestors. Their work was meant for the good to flourish, and his children carry on through his word. There is a light shining on the presence of evil. It is renewal through God, and the strong moral stance of my brothers and sisters in this little Wisconsin town and reservation community, on which we thrive and grow.

Lori J. Taguma
LCO Reservation, 2019
American Studies, Bachelor of Arts Thesis
University of California, Berkeley, 1999

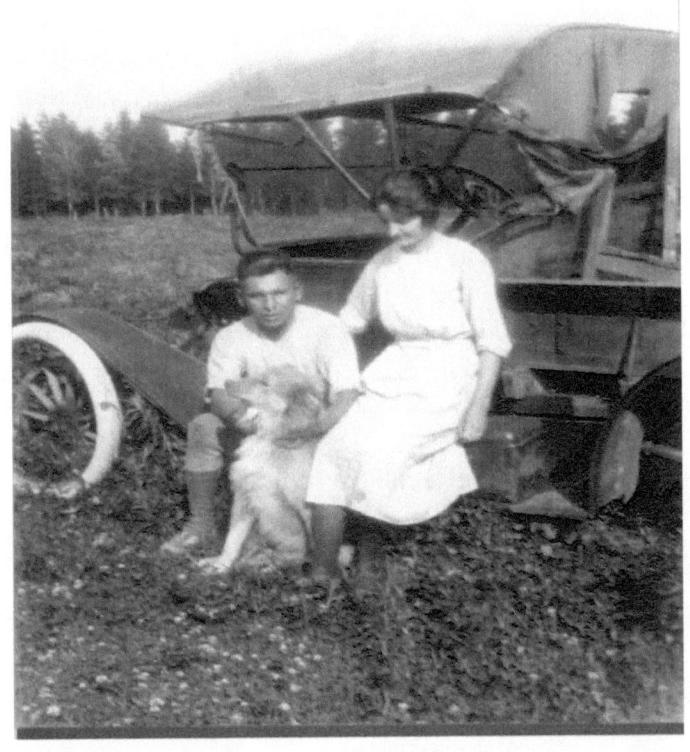

My grandparents, John and Bernadette Bracklin, on their
Whitefish allotment homestead, at Lac Courte Oreilles in the
1930's.

Introduction: Contextual Imagery

This is a discussion about the formation of Native American representations in the racialization (class formation) of U.S. culture. Within the context of this theme, I will discuss the medium of film, and examine the historical process of shaping Indian filmic imagery, including documentary images and current independent forms. (topics still pertinent today in 2019)

In defining the effects of film technique and semiotics, I will discuss the signification behind realistic models of Indians, and hope to reveal the meaning of portrayals within the context of broader socio-economic policies and goals. While exploring the topic of stereotypic Indian imagery, I will discuss the significant social and cultural challenges which independent Indian producers face, in shaping their symbolic images with an underlying sense of historic and temporal reality (reality as art). Issues to explore include the nature of native identity in American culture, Hollywood filmic representations of natives, and the new model of Indian imagery currently being created by natives about themselves.

Now that we (native people) are inventing our own commercial film narratives, we can elevate our view through filmmaking. The realistic trend in commercial native representation includes a change in tone, style, and substance which influences social conditions, policy and life for natives. A shift in artistic style now reveals a relatively conservative, political, and self-definitive view which no longer compromises the identity of native people. Indians are now creating realistic imagery by melding technical ability with modern forms, textured by social vision that liberates and intentionally promotes social transformation, beyond singular purposes of entertainment and away from darker hierarchal forms. Indigenized sites of transformation now reflect the shifting reality of native people, incorporating the traditional and historical context of our culture.

The recent proliferation of non-stereotypical, reflexive imagery suggests that Indians are talented, intelligent, and capable of bringing unique symbolic substance to modern American culture, in addition to presenting a challenge to the capitalist ethic underlying the Hollywood studio system. The new native imagery suggests a union of the best and the worst of both native and non-native worlds, representations shaped with the discipline, talent, and artistic technical ability of Indian filmmakers.

Representations of Indians have appeared within the range of commercial film genres since the inception of the cinema. Indian images were used as a tool by the dominant culture, one of several techniques designed to designate social acceptance for Native Americans (true as well for other people of color) within the larger American culture.

Art reflected life for natives, but from a biased and undulating point of view. In commercial film genres, Indians have portrayed noble savages in Western epics, acted as lead characters in Disney cartoons, and signified equally unreal constructions as aliens in science fiction dramas, with underlying social implications. During the cold war era, they represented the perceived threat of communism signified by "propagandist imagery seen in John Ford's cavalry in <u>The Searchers</u> *(1956),* where non-Indian, blue eyed actors represented Indian characters". [1] However, new language and imagery emerging from within the native culture, combined with new economic and technical resources, is reinventing consciousness of Native America.

---

1 Gonsalves, Ken, UCB Reader, November 1998.

Independent native film imagery is now linked culturally to the history of Indian people, shaped with detailed accounts of personal tragedies and achievements, revealing links to the larger political realm. Native filmmakers are combining subjectively entertaining elements with socially relevant documentary topics, adding new issues to pictures.

Although native images have been stereotyped for different reasons, the new commercial aesthetic develops the beauty and sovereignty of native identity. The new Indian film genre fills the gap between low budget, socially conscious documentary films created within native worldview, and the unrealistic yet entertaining large budget Hollywood film genre. New imagery reveals an intimate look at cultural constructs which consider the difference between several worlds and envisions the future.

Native Americans have attempted to elevate our social status in American culture by employing our philosophical style of reasoning and sense of subjectivity. In an effort to portray a sense of our reality, we continue to change representational policies and to provide our own interpretations. We persist in establishing social and economic stability for tribal members and in presenting our history truthfully, reflecting the "innate thoughts, traditions, and complimentary reasoning which shapes our semantic universe."[1] Mapping historically progressive models of the self in media discourse is especially significant, primarily to native life, a reconnection to one's identity.

Native writer Simon Ortiz describes native discourse as "a way of life, as perception, expression. Language is all expansive; the oral tradition in all its qualities and dimensions."[3] The condition of the spoken word refers to life, and utterances become "modifications of a total situation which is more than verbal."[4] During my conversations with members of the Lac Courte Oreilles Ojibway Tribe, (focus group, 1997) people expressed concern with establishing and maintaining economic stability, quality healthcare, and educational resources. But their primary interest was in maintaining a solid *traditional, idealistic* cultural foundation, qualities symbolized by our realistic native images.

Although Indian definition was delineated by dominant social methods in the past, those standards are being challenged by native development, including a means to create our own commercial film imagery. Tribal members at LCO, as well as members of other tribes, have

---

[1] Lac Courte Oreilles Focus Groups, Hayward, WIS, August 1997.
3 Ortiz, Simon, American Indian Writers Speak, Winged Words, page 107.
4 Orality and Literacy, page 101.

taken proactive positions by being positive, effective native role models. In a renewed era of self-determination, native people are creating self-definitive, artistic representations which embody underlying political, cultural, and emotional views.

Within native film culture, Indian writers, directors, and actors are shaping new images for the big screen designed to extract their mystery. Because individual meanings are entwined in the "genre and the unconscious spirit" [2] of the filmmaker, natives are now employing subjective, personal perspectives which provide the reality of native experience, replacing outdated cultural models and creating a new cinematic genre.

It has been said that Hollywood reinvents the Indian every year, but natives are now expressing localized native ideology within self-reflective "art" film models. There are several ways of "seeing" through the filmic lens, but audiences shape their perspectives around the effects. Realistic Indian auteur interpretations lie within the realm of "objective realism," where native body language, linguistic and musical code provides emotional subtext. Expanded, personalized authorial range embodies sensitized, meaningful gaze, a connection to one's surroundings and

---

[2] Steiger, Janet, Interpreting Film, page 120.

consciousness. New native filmic images shape boundaries of identity and reveal personal moments of transformation, baring underlying illusions. Representations now include a social vision which is beyond fetish, revealing a view which has become an exercise in eloquence, compassion, and brutal honesty.

Current Native American auteur interpretations "make an enormous effort to tell the truth in a realistic yet poetic way,"[6] by subtly revealing underlying spiritual and political codes representing native characters. Additionally, American audiences have positively responded to adjunct film representations and the relative shift in commercially representative filmic devices. The modern network of native communication (including local native newspapers, art and gaming journals, faxes, the internet, satellites, television, film) has facilitated the exchange of ideas between previously isolated tribes, connecting the rural with the urban cultural milieu. The enhanced path between the two worlds has influenced the static, patriarchal nature of Indian cinematic representations, which are now evolving into a *culturally enriching,*

---

6 Steiger, Janet, Interpreting Film, page 67.
7 Bordwell, David, Making Meaning, page 2.
8 Jones, Dan, American Indian Film Festival Interview, San Francisco, 1997.

entertaining model. New film images reconnect people with natural processes by either "duplicating the experience, or organizing the world for the spectator."[7] New native depictions now highlight conditions in rural and urban worlds, enhanced by fundamental political, cultural, and spiritual foundations. It is an evolutionary, candid view featuring personalized constructs which embody class, gender, and humanistic issues which define native culture.

In *American Scene* (1997), native producer Dan Jones takes a satirical gaze at stereotypic Indian images in Hollywood films. "The most interesting aspect of native film making is that some tribes now have their own money, allowing them to have creative control."[8] Awarded best documentary short at the American Indian Film Festival in 1997, his goal is to change commercial images of Native Americans simply because, "To continue the stereotyping is dangerous."[8]

Similarly, native writer Sherman Alexi, author of Indian Killer and the film *Smoke Signals (1997),* addressed the state of Indian images by announcing "My goal is to get Indians out of loincloths."[9] His primary role as a writer reflects a basic human argument, " I want to be known first as a writer. I am an Indian writer, talking about what I know."[9] His interpretations of native life are seen through a decidedly Cour D'Alene

16

'native filter', creating characters who are complex, sometimes humorous and brutally honest, reflecting deeply empathic emotions for Native Americans and other neglected groups, following eras of misrepresentation. I agree with his intention, stereotypic native film imagery is based largely in context and dialogue, not completely with buckskin costumes and mise-en-scene. The use of artistic, realistic dialogue combined with native direction, is essential in transcending the slapstick type of humor (usually politically self-effacing) used to formerly represent indigenous identity.

Smoke Signals renders realistic characters, and the work did receive audience acclaim as an "art" film, based on it's cinematic quality and descriptive story. The film provides a definitive artistic journey, and I applaud Sherman Alexi and the filmmakers, for providing a reflexive voice for a generation of young Native Americans. The film was entertaining, realistic, and groundbreaking. Please create more. It was pure genius.

Valerie Redhorse's <u>Naturally Native</u> *(1998)*, is also nearly successful in creating authentic humor. Her auteur vision portrays characters from a thoroughly modern native, feminine point of view. The film content is evolutionary and entertaining.

Naturally Native (1998) is the first commercial feature financed by the Mashantucket Pequot Tribe, which highlights the evolutionary and independent state of native cinema. Michael Dutton, Public Relations Director for the Pequot Tribe, notes a turning point for tribally financed film projects which will determine "Our continued financing of commercial film projects, depends on the success of the first." [10] Independent native feature filmmaking will evolve based on the cumulative experience and volume of native filmmakers who create work in all genres.

Native filmmaking is currently enhanced by the strength of the US economy and the stability of tribal economies. Combined with a national shift in democratic standards, the emerging native film genre weaves and highlights realistic beauty with political circumstances.

---

9   Alexi, Sherman, Sundance Film Festival Interview, 1997.
10   Dutton, Michael, Pequot Tribe, AI Film Finance Forum, SF, 1997.

The Cinematic History of Native Americans

> "The cinematic characterization of American Indians was perhaps one of the most destructive social forces used against native people, practically picking up where the cavalry left off."[11]

Although Native Americans have been involved with film culture since it's birth, involvement has typically been limited to following orders. Since the beginning of the cinema, natives have been represented within different genres and defined in "codes of illusion." Several early films created by Hollywood studios, such as D.W.Griffith's <u>The Redman and the Child</u> (1908),[12] were supportive of Native Americans but the perspective did not continue. The Hollywood machine fed the American audience persistently stylized visions of natives but failed to expose the "paradox of native identity."[12] Native objectification and symbolic elements of native cinematic representation reflected historical patterns, perpetuated audience desire, and defined social order.

Jean-Luc Goddard said that 'film was truth', but not now when everything is plausible. Intention and machinery are inextricably entwined.

---

11 Lori Taguma, <u>Native Americans in Cinema History,</u> Sundance Film Catalogue 1998.
12 University of California Berkeley, Media Library, 1997.
13 Barthes, Roland, <u>The Pleasure of the Text</u>, page 33.

Formation of images are borrowed and "governed by the image-reservoir of science, linguistically expressing the unconsciousness of the unconscious." [13]

Filmic images reflect the social hierarchy of different cultures, displayed frame by frame within the trajectory of individual desires. In the eyes and at the hands of Western filmmakers, Indian imagery has taken many forms, representations constructed mainly by auteur directors and studios who perpetuated elements of the "frontier myth" which signified a "cycle of regenerative violence".[3] In this genre, characters are involved in an eternal cultural struggle to either "conquor, repress, or defeat, which becomes an exercise in hierarchal formation."[4] Throughout the process of historical image development, Native American characters have been satirized, mythologized, commodified, and in different cycles, fetishized.

It was the impact of semiotics and realism which defined the "distance between stimulation and image," [5] necessary to transform our images and alter the events of past and future. Indian images devised by Hollywood standards came to represent *art as history or art as reality*. Film theorist Metz sees semiotics "not so much as a system of signification,

---

[3] Steadman, Raymond, Shadows of the Indian, page 135.
[4] Slotkin, Richard, Imagining Identities, page 39.
[5] Andrew, Dudley, Concepts in Film Theory, page 35.

as a *place* where various codes come together to create meaning".[6] Exposing images frame by frame through 'cultural filters' allows us to link the context of signifier and transformation, in the tradition or genre from which it comes. Perhaps the heightened artificiality with which Native Americans were depicted has increased our idealistic response.

Since no film reproduces reality, it is important to see "how a film is meaningful to the extent that it supports our semantic universe." Because different filmic genres "address social questions of human existence, within which elements and individual characterizations expose critical characteristics of culture and perspective,"[7] native representations have expanded beyond stereotypical boundaries of the western frontier and the reservation. Indian imagery of the 90's includes the urban world, "where 60% of Native Americans currently live."[8]

Modern social ideals are displayed in characterizations of Indian doctors, attorneys, artists, and single parents who combine traditional culture with modern identity. Independent Indian representations now promote a sense of belonging, for better or worse, to a community rooted in tribal culture and society largely by members who attempt to remain

---

[6] Ibid, page 68.
[7] Ibid, page 63.
[8] Sarris, Greg, UCLA Telephone Interview, 1997.

further uncontaminated by the chaos of urban America. New native filmic codes nearly signify reservations as oasises now that the frontier has been tamed, as a place to escape to from the larger chaotic American culture. Although is a rough unfinished oasis, the essence of the native world's beauty is reflected in it's paradoxical distress.

Sociologic View

This topic clearly shows the devastating effects which stereotypic imagery has had on the welfare of Native American people. Misleading historical representations ingrained in the consciousness of the American public need reformation, to include the diversity and the reality of Indian existence. Revealing important moments in current Native American history as well as correcting past misrepresentations, can lead to the shaping of efficacious social policies as well as spawning favorable representations. However, truth must be told.

I have frequently witnessed the need for realistic native imagery. While speaking with a fellow UC Berkeley student who would soon begin practicing international law, I found he was surprised to learn that I had been raised on a reservation, thinking that "all Indians lived in mud huts without running water."[9] Twenty years ago that was a common situation on Indian reservations. But my fellow student did not have a sense of present day 'modern Indians' or the influence of Indians in US history, including the fact that the first treaties were based upon U.S. government and Indian tribal law, both shaped by Iroquois Confederacy Statutes. The

---

[9] Personal Interview, UCB 1997.

majority of treaties between the US government and Indian tribes today remain virtually unfulfilled, hidden in the shadows of American history. My fellow UCB student's cynicism toward Indians is embedded in the immediacy of unrealistic media images which support the dominant hierarchy in American culture.

Realistic Indian images reflect detailed native identity, including a tribe's unique legal and economic status in U.S. culture. Filmic images perpetuate intimate psychological and social values as well as signify relationships with the government. Most importantly, Indian representations reveal a standard of democratic action and power underlying the social fabric within the political system. The shaping of positive, idealistic native images is in the best interest not only of the First Americans, but for all people of color who are concerned with just treatment in the U.S. system, signifying the nature of American culture. On an individual level, realistic representation is based in self-discovery for generations of Native Americans whose parents and grandparents were the victims of genocide, including mine. We, as well as other people of color, define liberating patterns of social meaning through our economic, intellectual, and cultural exchanges.

Since Indians in America occupy a uniquely sovereign political status, native individuals have constitutional legal freedom to exorcise our religious beliefs as well as our economic rights under federal law. In American culture, identity is defined and perpetuated by mass produced images, the effects unquestionably biased. Recent television campaigns propagandizing Indian gaming, reveals the political manuevering between the Nevada casino monopoly and select California tribes who currently operate casinos on reservations. The politicizing of the Nevada casino monopoly, is focused on denying tribes their sovereign economic rights. If they succeed in swaying public opinion against tribes who presently operate casinos, the legal precident would allow and tribal gaming laws, to favor corporations. (1999) The solution to all tribally based business, is sovereign economic development on reservations, and job training for all tribal members with financial oversight by the members, not just a few. (2019)

Although a larger portion of Native Americans now have access to the media, it was limited access to television production and the expensive medium of film which set standards for highly stylized interpretations. Armed with the tools of the medium, Indians are now prepared to counter negative media images with our version of the truth. Technical imaging has become a liberating modern form of Indian resistance. But there is also a problem created by the misuse of media tools used by gang members and drug dealers on reservations, who have infiltrated reservation communities, and misused sovereign territories, which counters the good from within and diminishes the culture. (2019)

In our evolving world of imagery, we determine our identities through interlocking points of varying difference. Roland Barthes expressed the process of shaping identity in terms of, "Culture, recurring as an edge between urban, political views of a class, where the traditions of our words and semiotic codes collide,"[10] producing many issues and perspectives to explore. Sociologically, genres "address questions of human existence"[11] within which critical characteristics of culture, beliefs and perspective are exposed through individual characterization.

In the mechanism of film representation, native imagery has come to symbolize the climate of redefinition, with inherent visions of memory. Personalized stories tied to native characterizations were rare before the Cold War era. Now native film technique largely employs methods of existential questioning, internalized significations visualized through

---

[10] Barthes, Roland, The Pleasure of the Text, page 32.
[11] Andres, Dudley, Film Theory, page 109.

themes representing cultures within cultures, spirituality versus capitalism, boundaries within boundaries. Aerial shots consistently define Indian territory and reservation boundaries in <u>Thunderheart</u> (1994), Disney's <u>Pocohontas</u> (1996), and in Alexi's <u>Smoke Signals</u> (1998). Spirituality is defined as animistic and native in Disney's <u>Pocohontas</u> (1996), as well as in Greg Sarris' <u>Grand Avenue</u> (1996).

In current Native American imagery, spiritual 'magic' is now inscribed by the God-Author presence of Indian writers and artists who reveal the artifice, in addition to the realistic portions of their filmic images. Through the, "cinematic apparatus and social institution"[12] which viewing film provides, we are "preconditioned to link film and dreams,"[13] determined by the intimate details of our private and public lives.

In the film <u>Smoke Signals</u> (1998), director Chris Eyre shapes the animated, magical essence of Thomas Builds the-Fire's character as spiritual medium, with a subtle soundtrack. Characters who lack social conscience are exposed by flat lighting and a similarly mundane sound track, the interactions woven with several musical voices.

Our cultural differences can be seen within the framework of film,

---

[12] Ibid, page 139.
[13] Ibid, page 141.

where art and unconscious desire meet, reflecting our public awareness and the spirit of the filmmaker. In <u>Smoke Signals</u> (1998), Thomas Builds-the-Fire represents the culmination of hope, righteousness, and renewal through faith, in a stark reservation environment. The current trend in independent native filmmaking reveals didactic, entertaining, subjectively realistic imagery.

Our differing viewpoints are reflected in our objective and subjective representations, expressed in language, and embodied in imagery: "The violent edge, the compromise brought about and the seam, which is erotic."[14] Historically in mass culture, native women were defined as the object of desire and native men were labeled violent and dangerous. But Indian people, especially traditional elders, have despised being objectified in dominant discourse and the media. Ishi, last tribal member of the Southern Yana and subject of extensive anthropologic study, refused to reveal his sacred name and self to non-tribal members in 1911. As 'Last of the Yahi', he signified a "simulation in absence of tribal names." Ishi deemed those who studied him as "Knowing many things, and much that is false. But he knew nature, which is always true."[1516] As last

---

[14] Barthes, Roland, <u>The Pleasures of the Text</u>, page 32.
[15] Ibid, page 25.
[16] Omi, Michael and Winant, Howard, <u>Racial Formation in the United States</u>, page 57.

of his tribe, Ishi's beliefs became a "literary construction, used to replace rather than represent Indian reality."[26] Indians have revealed much about their existence cross culturally for educational purposes, although being objectified within the larger social hierarchy for entertainment purposes was not part of our collective agenda.

For Native Americans, personalizing historical and cultural interpretations is important for a number of reasons but mainly because, "Recognition of the racial dimension in social structure is to interpret the meaning of race."[27] Unreal Indian images created by Hollywood auteur directors, were countered by didactic, grassroot native documentary projects, fundamentally educational and historical although limited in distribution. But a new form of native iconography has taken shape in the 1990's. These feature films provide realistic acting, entertaining story lines, and a satisfying sense of pleasure derived through ironic and frequently humorous depictions of native life. They personify a change in the way indigenous people see themselves, as well as provide realistic insight about our lives.

Greg Sarris' *Grand Avenue(1996)*, Sherman Alexi's *Smoke Signals (1998)*, Shirley Cheechoo's *Silent Tears (1998)*, and *Valerie Redhorse's Naturally Native (1998),* are the genesis of the new commercial Indian film genre. Now that we are directing, producing, and shaping our artistic visions where discourse and acting are central, we can participate in the social dialogue with self imposed values. The new native aesthetic resists commercially, "reductive classifications which obscure the processes of change and transformation."[17]

Since a compelling film is an "interpretation and an underlying promise of a different sort of knowledge and wisdom,"[18] the new Indian aesthetic now provides an objective, expressive model. Unconscious desire and perspective combine to portray *reality as art,* similarly as "classical film theory changed from historical to an art form."[19] The new native perspective is changing commercial Indian film imagery from representations of "chaos and meaninglessness, to a self-sustaining structure, as a process of transformation."[20] The shaping of the image as

---

[17] Foucault, Michel, University of California Berkeley Lecture, 1996.
[18] Andrew, Dudley, Film Theory, page 155.
[19] Ibid, page 150.
[20] Ibid, page 154.

filmic device presents cinematic representations as a, "permeable meta-narrative of a problem being worked on in the general cultural domain."[21]

Within native worldview many elders have expressed a desire to correct misperceptions about the Indian culture. Respected healer Max Bear, as well as other native elders have asked me to, "Bring your camera equipment. Let us tell our story."[22] Historically, native people have known that reflexive commercial imagery as well as documentary messages created by Indians about themselves resonate with truth.

An acute awareness and development of the subconscious is new to native imagery in the 1990's. Dream imagery recreates memory, an important element of this 'art' film model. Personalized narration is combined with symbolic cultural codes. This type of tone and interpretation, "makes an enormous effort to tell the truth in a realistic yet poetic way."[23] The new native film genre provides realistic acting and entertaining story lines with ironic, frequently humorous depictions of native life. Newly fashioned native imagery creates Indian heroes out of

---

[21] Steiger, Janet,Interpretating Film, page 257.
[22] Interview, Kyle, South Dakota, 1993.
[23] 34 Film Interpretations, page
260.

everyday characters through introspective, empathic views. The new look is imperfect but defines boundaries and gaps from the native perspective.

Feminine characters are primary to the new native aesthetic, providing modern ideals of beauty, justice, and strength characterized with a fluid sense of rhythm and elegance, at odds with the genocide of the past. The new sense of native beauty is heightened in its naturalness, but combined with a realistic sense of knowledge and creativity. Native male characters act as saviors in physical conflict, but native women negotiate and provide the long-term solutions, remaining somewhat stereotypic although the genre has evolved.

There are several ways of shaping filmic images. But it is within the shaping of images as filmic device where Merleau-Ponty described his modernist post-Gestalt view as: "A process by which my body entertains shifting yet organized relations to that which is outside it."[24] Theorists Bazin and Kraucauer believe that, "there is little essential difference between perception in the cinema and the world at large, extending rather than altering perception." [25]33 Mitry's psychology takes on a,

> "constructive rather than a receptive function of the eye, believing that cinema's quasi-natural perceptual base distinguishes it from all

---

[24] Andrew, Dudley, <u>Film Theory</u>, page 34.
[25] Ibid, page 19.

other art forms, which is why it is at once an aesthetics and a psychology of cinema."[26]

Marxist theorists see centered representations as a way of "replacing the representations of cosmic and religious space, of cultivated landscapes ruled over by proprietors, where the spectator is master of the universe," [27] which is where native and non-native ideology meet and provide conflict. Social theorist Pierre Bourdeau, in addition to those in the native world know,

"that social autonomy, statements of truth, access to the media, as well as cross cultural engagement,"[28]

adds collective social value, surpassing mere artistic license and objectivity. And in historical film philosophy, spectatorship creates meaning as Andre Bazin argues,

> "classical film theory arose from a historical situation to an art form, changing the world from chaos and meaninglessness to a self-sustaining structure, as a process of transformation." [29]

In current native cinematic displays, underlying cultural values can be seen emerging from the sentiments of Hollywood, establishing a diminished commercialized foundation and legitimizing the native

---

[26] Ibid, page 19.
[27] Ibid, page 23.
[28] Bourdeau, Pierre, Lecture, University of California, Berkeley 1996.
[29] Steiger, Janet, Iterpretating Film, page 37.

experience. Images are exposed frame by frame through 'cultural filters', allowing us to link the context of signifier and transformation, to the genre or tradition from which it comes. Although Native American images resonate with autonomous intentions, it is the audience who has identified with natives and spirituality, who have overcome the challenges of genocide and economic disparity.

Artists are here for the public to shape, cut, and fashion labels with reflections of honesty and truth. But where is the line between self-expression, social engineering and truth. The medium of cinema coupled with social, political, and cultural 'filters', mediates reality for us. The signifier is, "tied to a particular and singular mental concept underlying several directorial intentions: either to entertain, to build morale, to escape reality, or to support values,"[30] uniting spectators around the effects.

The intimacy of the theater allows a personal conversation to take place between viewer, screen, and collective audience. Film spectatorship consists of unlocking the hidden, manipulated codes of symbolic abstraction and implicit imagery, in which our social and cultural criteria are framed. Cinematic representations reflect the ways in which we see, linking our definitions of signifier and self.

---

[30] Andrew, Dudley, Film Theory, page 40.

In *Smoke Signals* *(1997)*, the third film which I will look at, Indian author and director define their perspectives through film technique, empathically delineating cultural differences and highlighting representational elements which signify native identity. The second film, *Dance Me Outside* *(1994),* combines native actors with reservation mise-en-scene, but authorial voice and direction is non-native. Both films provide characterizations which utilize the "difference between film and reality,"[31] fashioning a progressively realistic native image. The first film, Disney's Pocohontas (1994), is purely non-native but based on several historical characters.

As with literature, the shift from film as a medium of recording, to film as an *art form*, mimicked and distorted beyond the 'significance' of a single image. With the introduction of the first motion picture, the genesis of a new revealing art began as "a business, as cultural product and commodity, and as machinery."[32] The resultant "unity of action", reflects the ability of an artist in combining the poetic elements of scenes, in achieving narrative continuity and intention. Disney's *Pocahontas* (1994) is a prime example of a native story told with a paternalistic entertainment 'filter'. It

---

[31] Arnheim, Rudolph, <u>Film As Art</u>, page 42.
[32] Mast, Gerald, <u>A Short History of the Movie</u>, page 45.

exemplifies an European reading of Indian bodies. Undeniably, definitions of biologic and cultural superiority are displayed throughout pictorial art history. The history of film exhibits scientific realism, from which cinematic narrative has evolved as an art form. But there is no pure science without effects. The evolution of, "narrative and normative representations seen in individual films, genres and periods," [33] reflects a shift from *realism used to document*, to signification of, "modern aestheticism," in film theory.

Since Native Americans are now creating our own feature length cinematic displays, sentiments are based on foundations of knowledge and legitimized with inherently internalized representations, creating a less commercialized, deeply personal look in native imagery. In addition to knowing that 'no aesthetic is pure', we know that it is possible to alter the events of past and future with technical impact. If form determines the decadence of art, then the underlying cultural values in Native American ideology, are affecting the rules of historical film practices. Our style of reasoning is effectively objectifying native imagery and the sensibilities of educated, creative audiences by offering an alternative to the fantastic forms of Hollywood. Stylistic links continually emerge from Hollywood.

---

[33] Ibid, page 66.

An Indian recently invaded space as a passenger on the Startrack ship Voyager, although the character is unfortunately still romanticized and lacks three-dimensional depth.[34]   But it provides pure entertainment.

Modernism has lent a hand in constructing reality by "forcibly rearranging our very ways of processing meaning."[35] In addition to the darkness and space in which the theater audience interacts with the screen, the use of filmic devices in shot, reverse-shot sequence are used to build suspense and to distance, the mise-en-scene is used to frame and slow motion, black and white film exhibits dream vision and temporality. Additionally film technique includes the effects of,

> "vraisemblance, the versimilar or seeming-real, the comfortable feeling of reality, surrounding the significations of images whenever they pan or cut to an object of character's expression, *indicating inter-linked connection to the spectator's* world,"[36]

add to the new native aesthetic.   Few cultures reinvent the audience for themselves as Native Americans have. The emergence of independent native film forms, are changing the face of the cultural landscape. Perhaps our role as mediator between earthly and spiritual domains serves to teach lessons in morality, forgiveness, and justice, opposing our role as target

---

[34] Hill, Richard, Why I Hate Star Trek, Aboriginal Voices Magazine, November 1998.
[35] Andrew, Dudley, Film Theory, page 62.
[36] 47 Ibid, page 64.

for many years. But there is more to mapping historic native representation as a practice, including defining evolving indigenous models of the self. Audiences have also changed what they want to hear. To get to the issues, artists have taken different approaches, adding new points of identity, melding traditional aspects with the new in creating sensitivity and a richness to life.

Within these different genres and unique points of view, I define the elements which have changed native representation to it's present highlighted form. First I will discuss the brief history of Indian representation in American film culture.

Native Americans in Film History

Films have played a major role in shaping the psychological and moral landscape of America. With the introduction of the cinema in 1895, different cinematic forms evolved, encompassing elements which comprised another "medium's version of reality, swallowed by members of that culture and workings of ideology."[37] The voracity of moving images over print images created endless possibilities through manipulation of

---

[37] Andrew, Dudley, Film Theory, page 63.

elements, diminishing the truth, affecting the psychology of the population, and raising moral doubts.

Within the 'ideology of the dominant class', where French artist Roland Barthes presumed "the text needs it's shadow: a *bit* of ideology, a *bit* of representation, a *bit* of subject: ghosts, pockets, traces, subversion must produce it's own chiaroscuro,"[38] generalizations of native character have embodied different identities to capture imaginations. Constructions of natives represented fear of the unknown seen as the primitive, dying savages in *Wild Bill Hickcock* (1938) and characters embodied public policy issues of the 50's in <u>Broken Arrow</u> (1950). Post-60's activism changed natives to heroes in *Billy Jack* (1971), and during a new era of technology native women's roles represented the primitive, sexually charged Princess of the 70's, 80's, & 90's, culminating in Disney's <u>Pocahontas</u> (1994). As urban Americans lost touch with their traditional cultures, native imagery represented a narrow view of spirituality lost. The image finally expanded into positive, slightly romanticized yet realistic native characters in *Dances With Wolves* (1994).

Why were some images of Native Americans so agreeably accepted, while at the same time some were not? In D.W. Griffith's first

---

[38] Ibid, page 81.

western, *The Redman and the Child* (1908) a white boy and young Indian were depicted in an 'enduring friendship'. But by the 1950's, cold war film culture reflected the political climate of the era, signifying Indian imagery as public policy problems in an escapist effort to build national morale. As industrialization and urban life took it's toll and people distanced themselves from natural, harmonious rhythms, they began to respond to native worldview with increasing degrees of acceptance in American culture. Subsequent portrayals of natives in the cinema altered social perception as audiences responded to the spiritual, earthy nature of realistic native life. The shifting hierarchy can be seen today although the pace is slow.

In commercial film culture, leading Indian roles have historically been portrayed by non-Indians, such as Raquel Welsh in The Legend of Walks Far Woman (1983). Since Jay Silverheels played the role of Tonto, the 'noble savage' to Clayton Moore's, The Lone Ranger *(1947),* native images were fraught with restrictive directorial bias and depicted with a romanticized view. John Wayne's portrayal of a 'racist Indian hater' in The Searchers (1956) defined the market for western themes in 1950's cold war America, reflecting the political climate, portraying Indians as "vanishing Americans".[39] And especially for native women, the trends and "cliches seem to be irresistable."[40]

In the 90's legendary characters Pocahontas and Hiawatha, were similarly redefined as was the language of logistical expression. Native culture was reenvisioned and characters became hyper-real. Disney's Pocahontas, (1994) caricaturized and desexualized images of Indians as fetishistic constructions, transforming natives into personifications of the real, culminating in the satirical mythic images seen in HBO's embarrassing farce, Hiawatha (1996). Audience response to the overtly romanticized script was unsympathetic. In response, a new version of Hiawatha's story is being written which encompasses a heroic, realistic native perspective (1998).[41]

It has been said that every ten years a great Native American novel is published or a breakthrough film is released which changes dominant stereotypes. However, native people are still awaiting the creation of a commercially successful Indian theme film which will shatter stereotypes and change attitudes. What has hindered the production of the realistic Indian aesthetic?

---

[39] Steadman, Raymond, Shadows of the Indian, page 113.
[40] Green, Rayna, Native American Women 1983, page 1.
[41] Tinkerman, Randy, Hiawatha Screenwriter, 1998.

Since contact with Europeans in 1492, and especially since Buffalo Bill's Wild West Show (1931), it has been said that Native American imagery acts as a "barometer of multicultural relations,"[42] in American culture. Created with the artistic license of Hollywood, Indian images portraying 'vanishing Americans' became romanticized reality in the new frontier era. Commercial expression and critique were largely limited by dominant political and corporate powers, the filtering process reflecting social agendas and political backlash. But what critical elements define and shape Indian imagery?

With the invention of the camera by Frenchman Louis Jacques Daguerre in 1839, as with the first native images shaped by Edward S. Curtis in 1839, Native American identity has assumed several politically charged dimensions, encompassing sites of genocide, struggle, and reflected unconscious desire. Labels were generally constructed and images recorded as representational shadows on the changing American landscape. Although Edward S. Curtis was a brilliant pictorialist and the first to record native life on the western frontier, the nature of native ideology presented was incomplete and stylized, subjected to a biased pictorial and ideological perspective.

---

[42] Sarris, Greg, Personal interview, 1997.

Edward Curtis was the

"prime documentarian of Indian life between 1896 and 1930, during which time he collected interviews and original Indian stories."[54]

He was known as a historian and his work reflected "definitive photography, as well as deep identification with the plight of the American Indian and their deep abiding faith in the mystery of life." [54]

But the entirety of Curtis' construction was skewed by distance and angle between signifier and denotation, "that which the signifier depicts."[55] Although Curtis' native subjects were frequently eager to reveal and record certain details of their lives were deemed sacred. His work defined Native America for a time as the "single recorded history" of native life but presented a partial reality, depicting incomplete recreations of Indian life. parts of their lives, superficial aspects of their dress, ceremony, and myths,

From the moment Curtis and his financial backer, industrialist financier J.P. Morgan, began representing Indians in twenty text volumes of <u>The North American Indian</u> 1907-1930, natives were portrayed with a romanticized view. This standard was also apparent in filmic imagery, when

[54] Curtis, Edward S., <u>Prayer to the Great Mystery</u>, page 81. [55] Andrew, Dudley, <u>Film Theory,</u> page 71.
[56] Curtis, Edward, S. <u>Prayer to the Great Mystery,</u> page 81.

photographs were used to represent increasingly ambiguous ideas. *In the Land of the War Canoes: Kwakiutl Indian Life on the Northwest Coast* (1914) and *The Shadow Catcher: Edward S. Curtis and the North American Indian* (1974), the "photographer, anthropologist, and filmmaker presents Indian life using 10,000 songs, 40,000 pictures, interviews, and original stories"[56] Again, it was the audience's humanistic response to Curtis' work which heightened interest in Native Americans.

Since the birth of the cinema, Indian images have been labeled with layers of subtext in mainstream American culture, shaped by non-native hands. Native American characters have been satirized, mythologized, commodified, and in different cycles, sympathized. The proliferation of "Indian sympathy films in the 1990's, is attributed to the popularity of Kevin Costner's, Dances With Wolves, (1991)."[57] The film portrays natives with traditional tribal language and dress, but continues to romanticize the native perspective. How do the elements of native cinematic discourse signify, define the desire of audience and social order?

We know that cultural identity is not static, but in the realm of image making it was the adoption of the "art" film which became a catalyst for realistic Native American characterization, in which complex identities

57 Rollins, Peter, The Hollywood Indian, page 2.

began to resonate with "objective realism". The "art" film changed expectations by presenting an alternative view to illusionary, stereotypic Hollywood imagery. It is important to look at the historical impact of Native American signification within both genres, as well as the effects of predetermined knowledge upon audience response, to understand socially significant native cultural models. Additionally, how the nature and development of the "art" film corresponds to sites of Native American cinematic evolution in American history.

Many native writers and artists, including Pulitzer Prize recipient Scott Momaday, whose book and film House Made of Dawn (1968), stressed the importance of authentic representation as, "the act of language creating the consciousness of man."[43] Serious moral issues concerning Native Americans had not been packaged for the American viewing audience before that time. Ortiz's account of the urban alienation which natives experienced during the 1950's and 1960's, added new realistic, dramatic elements to commercial native representations. His personalized exploration sentimentalized issues of relocation, displacement, and a reconnection to one's identity, exposing the devastating effects of cultural alienation to the American audience. He was also the first native author to

---

[43] Ortiz, Simon, Winged Words, page 107.

filmically portray the dehumanizing effects of the 1950's urbanization policy while employing native actors.

Native based satirical explorations followed slowly, filling a cultural gap where racist backlash toward Indians and other racial groups (especially Asians) prevailed during the Cold War era. When political paranoia subsided, Indian characters embodied the role of hero. The film Billy Jack (1971) set the stage for rural Indians and moral citizens to wage war against corrupt government officials and their capitalistic allies.

After the Cold War era, traditional native culture was sequestered on reservations, as the influx of different groups into the urban milieu created a homogenized industrialized society. In response to US government boarding school assimilation and relocation techniques, Native Americans vehemently protected their cultural beliefs and spirituality. Native histories currently being recreated show the effects of genocide through boarding school horror stories, cultural alienation, alcoholism, and recovery based on a strong spiritual bond.

During the post war era, existentialist roles were seen in independently produced cinema. In Powwow Highway (1988), protagonist Philbert, played by Gary Farmer, engages the question of being Indian. In this genre, characters struggle to reconstruct their identities, yet they are caught between internalized racial stereotypes, religious conflict, and politicized labels. In the short history of native filmmaking the compelling, realistic characterizations have been financed by liberal independent companies.

Self-actualization and multicultural identity are the basis for Thunderheart 1992), in which a native woman played by Shiela Tousey, finally portrays the lead native female character. Val Kilmer (mixed race) successfully portrayed a young half-breed FBI agent who explores his cross-cultural perspective, spurning a return to his lost spiritual heritage. Hollywood did not allow Indian men to portray themselves in lead roles until the rush for realistic Indian portrayals followed Dances with Wolves, which spawned the trend toward historically accurate, sympathetic native themes employing native language and lead characters. In HBO's Lakota Woman (1994), UCLA Professor Hanay Gigeomah directed female native actress Irene Bedard in a commercial project that had far greater independent vision, dimension, and reflexive self-perception. Again, native film projects supported by independent production companies historically provide greater intellectual entertainment.

However, as Indian economic stability has developed on a national level, the quality of life for native people has improved, including our methods of communication. The medium is the message for Indian artists who master the technology and process of filmmaking, significantly shaping new images by employing native writing, acting, and directing. Greg Sarris's <u>Grand Avenue</u> (1996), Sherman Alexi's <u>Smoke Signals</u> (1997), Valerie Redhorse's <u>Naturally Native</u> (1997), and Shirley Cheechoo's independent Canadian production, <u>Silent Tears</u>(1997), are created with an increasingly native core. The HBO television movie, <u>Grand Avenue,</u> (1996) focused on urban Indian women and cross-cultural relations, lending an objective 'native mirror' to the characterization of contemporary native life.

Valerie Redhorse's <u>Naturally Native</u> *(1997)*, is the first tribally funded feature which portrays a new sense of native beauty, heightened in its naturalness but combined with a realistic sense of knowledge and creativity. <u>Naturally Native</u> investigates the lives of several urban Indian women, revealing the consequences of their actions. The structure of the genre is designed to create anticipation and to prove or disprove aspects of cultural beliefs. Much of the new native genre contains aspects of the noir structure. The femme fatale model is expanded to include variations of the dangerous feminine protagonist, although women are not completely portrayed as martyr.

Canadian artist Shirley Cheechoo's <u>Silent Tears,</u> is a true story of personal struggle which resonates completely with native identity. Directed by Cheechoo, the film highlights her family's struggle for survival during a long winter in the outback and recreates the complex operation which her mother performed to save her father's life. The heightened technical quality and content of these films raise the bar for the next cycle of dramatic native feature films, in addition to increasing audience expectations.

Depictions of natives in films are based on significant native writing, directing, and acting in conjunction with contemporary criticism. Film technique is used to define difference and determine the *cultural* elements through which native identity is signified and used to create tone.

Disney's <u>Pocohontas</u> *(1994)* is a story framed in cartoon structure. Freudian filmic conventions are used to create the patriarchal *femme fatale* model in <u>Pocahontas,</u> which alters the ultimate reality. The second film, <u>Dance Me Outside</u> *(1994)*, ties native actors to nuance, inflection, and reservation mise-en-scene. I will look at how the trickster coyote character negotiates cross-cultural relations in melodramatic slapstick style, using

49

non-native direction and discourse. In Smoke Signals (1997), native signification provides the context and significance of dream imagery, flashbacks, and historic religious impact on native culture. Meaning is portrayed through subjective, existentialist interpretation using modern Indian discourse and direction, delineating cultural differences and representational native elements.

The last two films reflect expressive, 'objective realism' within entertaining, slightly melodramatic storylines. They use contemporary filmic devices which relay unconscious desire and recreate memory from an increasingly native perspective. Smoke Signals utilizes a formula for subjective native characterization which constructs a, "difference between film and reality,"[44] with critical audience acclaim.

DISNEY'S POCOHONTAS (1994)

In the world of fiction it is imaginable to blur the lines of reality, but is history sacred? No, certain ideas predominate but each generation must take responsibility for creating fictive characters, imagery, and their history as myth or as reality. Disney's version of Pocahontas, combines the mythology of past eras with sexuality, sentimentality, and spectacle. As

---

[44] Arnheim, Rudolf, Film as Art, page 42.

the premier animation machine of Hollywood, Disney has taken timely advantage of social concerns, weaving issues of diversity and feminine power into marketing ploy. The current packaging of Pocahontas includes a dangerous, [59]heroic *femme fatale* character standardized in the spirit of Disney romance, who is:

> "a love object who poses a threat to the life, welfare, or psychological well being of a male protagonist. She is an articulation of fears surrounding notions of uncontrollable drives and fading of subjectivity. She is situated as evil and is often punished or killed."[60]

In 1990's commercial film culture, Pocahontas' caricature has embodied spiritual and geographic characteristics, transforming the imagery of her body. Her personality has engaged audiences for generations but the changing imagery of her myth has reflected varying versions of masculinity and femininity, defining race, class, and gender, revealing links to theatrical and literary evolution. In Disney's colonial construct, Pocahontas becomes a fetish at the intersection of all issues. She acts as an agent of absence and fear, practically transforming into the 'other' and almost transforming the 'other' into her cultural identity. In

---

[60] The Fatal Woman, page 2.
[61] Ibid, page 56.

Disney's version she represents the point of transformation, an intersection of constructions.

Theories based on reading iconographic codes have evolved with the development of narrative cinema. Several psychological theories of the unconscious including the work of Freud and Lacan relate underlying image formation. Most notably,

> "the conception of binary opposition as constituting language structure, producing specific subject conditions and psychic dynamics, such as phallocentrism, in a way that it becomes a feature of a social formation, not a biological or even cultural necessity." [61]

The image making machine of Hollywood and particularly the Disney culture, reflect patriarchal interpretations deeply rooted in Freudian ideals, defined by gender and class. Content is based on symbolism reflecting, "culture specific semantic charters which condition our thoughts and emotions."[45] The camera is not a passive receiver but is used as a device to conjour and project appearances in order to achieve desired effects. In this version of <u>Pocahontas,</u> the camera eye becomes voyeuristic observer and game hunter, constructing perspective, 'positioning' the subject while gazing at her catlike, free spirited actions, and then conquoring her. The

---

[45] Steiger, Janet, <u>Interpreting Film</u>, page 65.

Disney formula creates memorable imagery by repeating organized variations of historical discovery, while highlighting the difference "between film and real life, making formally significant images." [46] Disney's symbolism is different from native cultural forms which fill historical gaps with layers of self-discovery.

John Smith is painted as courageous conqueror of the new frontier. He materializes as significant link in Pocahontas's life 'dream', as savior in her unconscious trajectory of desire. Character and boundaries are established through juxtaposed parallel action shots in action, reaction sequence, delineating chemistry at contact, in addition to establishing the trajectory of the discourse. However, the true story of Pocahontas has been twisted in this discourse to support Disney's format. Shooting and editing technique also are part of the subject matter, reflecting form and content in screen as "the imaginary signifier." [47] Disney code. But the apparatus does not change, the viewer still sees the unconscious which takes on concrete forms. Lacanian theory, contoured by Freudian ideals, supports the "trajectory of pleasure", [65] which underlies clashing ideologies. In this

---

[46] Arnheim, Rudolph, <u>Film as Art</u>, page 42.
[47] Andrew, Dudley, <u>Film Theory</u>, page 35.

version of Pocahontas, conflict is portrayed through parallel editing technique, seen as the gap where " an *impediment relays unconscious discoveries* where incomplete solutions are formed."[66] However, the principle of desire "finds it's boundary crossing the threshold imposed by the pleasure principle." [67] Which is where notions of "religion, illusion and phantasty" are situated. In this film, Lacanian theory relates male motivation to underlying projections of repressed, unconscious male desire, laced in each cinematic frame and contoured with slight inclusions of independent female will, heightening the challenge to John Smith. Pocahontas' image embodies ideals of truth, virtue, and courage at the site of cultural clash but in this interpretation her image is coded with fantastic labels. She is labeled as the *femme fatale*, the causality of conflict, the object of desire, and dangerous liasion in this new world.

Ideologic devices are particularly framed in Disney's Pocahontas, highlighted by comic, unreal representations woven in modern discourse. Pocahontas the Indian Barbie doll, implicitly embodies ideals of cool shapely hillsides, lush fertile forests, flowing rivers, and free swirling hair. But audiences respond to her courageous femininity. The

---

[65] Steiger, Janet, Interpreting Film ,page 65.
[66] Lacan, Jacques, The Four Fundamental Concepts of Psycho-Analysis, page 25.
 [67] Ibid, page 31.

feminine form of protagonist Pocahontas is reflected symbiotically within the landscape, mimicked and 'pregnant with form'. Her colors and tone are portrayed as warm, earthy, natural yet her spirit is strong willed and feminist. She is countered by the antagonistic, colonial governor's tone who is over the top, his representation coded with melodramatic, comedic orange, pink, and blue tones as well as his supporting cast of man servant and bulldog. The extreme camera angles, combined with the animal characteristics and musical numbers, add slapstick aspects of comic relief, the few elements of their natures which are particularly funny. Disney films reflect a brilliant auteur's vision, whose patriarchal tone and format adapts slightly to address social concerns. In this version of Pocahontas, modernized images consisting of racially diverse characteristics are formed using various racial models.[48] The resulting assemblage embodies cool colors, stylistic, sexy poses and implicit diversity. In complimentary romantic style, John Smith's deeply chiseled features embody adventurous European aggression, his image emulating and juxtaposed with jutting

---

[48] Disney Animator Interview, 1997.

rocks and forward thrusting ships on which he is frequently poised. He is particularly framed by his huge gun which he frequently points at Pocahontas and the other 'savages'.[49] Pocahontas adds an element of confusion to John Smith's unconscious desire at first encounter. She appears out of the mist and water, as 'dream' imagery, her shape transcending from evil enemy into beautiful creature and 'surprising discovery' within seconds. Elements of film convention are used to stylize objectivity, "as a tool to serve the desire of artistic creation, characterizing the object in a particular sense and introducing an attractive element of surprise by the unexpected shapes which a familiar object can assume, leading the spectator beyond the sphere of ordinary human conceptions."[50]

In Lacan's version the "unconscious finds itself on the opposite side to love."[51] The undulating conflict and tension between desire and love creates the trajectory of the film, true also for femme fatale characterization. The couple's union is ill-fated, as are other male

---

[49] Rhetoric Interview, 1998.
[50] Arnheim, Rudolph, Film as Art, page 42.
[51] Lacan, Jacques, The Four Fundamental Concepts, page 25.

characters who are touched by Pocahontas's 'magic'. Disney's <u>Pocahontas</u> does provide a simplistically fashioned, diverse answer to the question posed by John Smith: "What is different about this new world?" As premier entertainment machine, Disney is known for commercially packaging current issues entwined in romantic notions. In this version historical discourse is redefined, shaping the Indian maiden into a mixture of victim and strong willed woman of the 1990's who chose her role as martyr. Diversity is filmically represented by the shifting colors of the wind, feminine wisdom is embodied by talking grandmother tree, but the hierarchy is apparent. The film is wonderfully crafted with beautiful, award winning music and artistic spectacle, but the meaning is deemed unreal.

Film discourse can be an educational tool, but when discourse is reengineered from a biased perspective continuously, effects are damaging. Antagonistic colonists painted Indian representations with the word 'savage', and the Indians' war song counters with a kinder definition of colonial 'savage'. But truth as a transformational tool is strictly patriarchal in this film. If the Disney version presented the true story of Pocahontas who was kidnapped, taken to England, and died a short time later, the moral would be unfulfilled and the tone of the film would be deemed realistic and inappropriate for it's young audience. Disney's <u>Pocahontas</u> does not fulfill the format of an 'art' film by reengineering historical fact. Acting and story line are largely unrealistic, told from a historically patriarchal point of view.

Each generation creates their history by re-discovering larger issues of the structure. But how can we know what to believe? We can find evidence, show possession in media images versus manipulation, depending on desired effect. For example, to re-create and mythologize what the *Indians* were thinking while Curtis captured their images, or to show what Pocahontas' life was like after she was kidnapped and taken to Europe by colonials. Modern values and conflict are woven into Disney's Pocahontas, using intertextual parallels between the governor and native chief, the dog and raccoon, Pocahontas and John Smith, mother nature and technology, implicit value of gold and corn, wisdom and greed. But the effects of the Disney myth will reach into the next generation because of the film's brilliant artistic technique.

The ideologic message in Disney's <u>Pocahontas</u> as cultural product goes beyond the effects of the 'gaze', using film as an art form to continue the "cyclical identification that perpetrates negative images at the same time attempting to transcend stereotypes,"[52] Film is based upon fictive

constructs and rhetorical framework where the,

> "formula for fictional constructions, decor, characterization, and
> photography which dominated film themes were based on ideas
> that worked before, and were bunched into cycles."[53]

Disney caricatures will most likely continue to perpetrate

unrealistic representations of natives until demographics demand change,

but native imagery in alternative genres has evolved to include images of

modern native people, where native and non-native cultures intersect. The

new native perspective is created by melding traditional culture with

modern forms resulting in interesting, significant cultural images which

express time and place. Storyteller artistry embodies self-definition as

author Gerald Vizenor attempts to,

> "Discover ourselves in the story as imaginative, to feel good about
> it, and imagine myself moving through certain contradictions and
> conflicts with good humor, maybe a lesson and without being
> damaged
> by it."[54]

Although native culture was labeled to recur as a 'fiction', an illusion,

---

[52] Rolling, Peter, Film and History, The Hollywood Indian, page 5.
[53] Mast, Gerald, A Short History of the Movies, page 228.
[54] Vizenor, Gerald, Winged Words, page 174.

the familiar made strange and fantastic by dominant ideology, native worldview has begun to encompass a vast oral storytelling tradition woven with tribal histories, unique humor and contemporary stories. The mythic function of Native America has changed. Indians have become self-definitive signifiers in new moral cultural characterizations, playing realistic roles and creating new forms of meaning within a wider spectrum of artistic genres. Several people from the Lac Courte Oreilles Reservation in northern Wisconsin saw little positive native imagery in Disney's _Pocahontas._[55] But the rural perspective varies slightly from the urban view. A Navajo woman working for the Disney Corporation insisted that her child positively identified with their portrayal of Pocahontas.[56] Although there is a gap between rural and urban perspectives, Indian people know that increasingly positive native representations will evolve as we conscientiously and consistently create realistic, entertaining imagery.

---

[55] Lac Courte Oreilles focus group participants, 1997.
[56] Native Americans in Film Arts interview, Los Angeles, 1996.

DANCE ME OUTSIDE (1994)

Among the many reasons for the change in native representation within our multicultural society, is a shift from the portrayal of the history of natives to contemporary, indigenous interpretation of native literature. New realistic media images created within the native culture provide a humility, an elegance, and a sensibility which has fueled and inspired a new generation of artists. Realistic images provide an alternative to negative, 'hostile media', including the impersonal, provocative images which are an antithesis to art. Indians needed to create realistic, classic media messages based on self-definitive discourse mainly because,

> "Native Americans, African Americans, Hispanic Americans, Asian Americans, are not just engaging in a parlor exercise--they are writing for their lives. And once these voices have been heard, there is no turning back."[57]

The impact of *identity art* is revealed by transformative moments, as indigenous writers relay the fears and motivations of their sources, affecting the attitudes of a new generation. Artistic identity similarly defines the dynamics of fiction, fantasy, and reality. In the Canadian film, Dance Me Outside *(1994)* indigenous agendas are relayed through native textured dialogue, decentralized narrative action, and modern native music.

---

[57] Native American Literature, page xi.

Details are woven through an existentialist, melodramatic soap opera framework, where native rhythms underlie native characters who deftly embody solutions to social challenges. Although the characters are slightly more developed than past characterizations their spiritual connection is textured with parody. The definitive difference between <u>Dance Me Outside</u> and Disney's <u>Pocahontas</u> is displayed in the increasingly realistic narrative conflict and community based native solutions, largely provided by feminine characters who embody heroic ideals but who are not completely martyrized. New packaging paints native characters as stylized, metamorphized icons who transcend projections of anger and mystery. The feminine characterizations go beyond the central femme fatale model, reflecting fashion, attitude, and language which suggests mature native women who are chic and intelligent.

Aspects of <u>Dance Me Outside's</u> *(1994)* story line fit melodramatic expectations in which "the good must be rewarded and the wicked punished, the 'latent' message of soap operas."[58] In the soap opera genre, frequently addressed social problems include the role of women in "familial disorder, where subplots reveal the moral fantasy underlying individual fates and the action is generated by attempting to keep the family

---

[58] Modeleski, Tania, <u>Loving With a Vengeance</u>, page 90.

together."[78]   Although male counterparts are "centered around a male

controlling figure with whom the spectator can identify,"[59][60] there is a

decentralization of characterization in the new native aesthetic which

allows the audience to identify with different "conflicts, egos, and

motivations."[79]   In this film, the definitive soap opera format is used to

characterize elements of life on many reservations which are essentially,

> "set in small towns and involve two or three families intimately
> connected with one another. Families are often composed of
> several generations, allowing a greater sense of intimacy and
> continuity, a greater audience involvement, and a sense of
> becoming a part of the lives and actions of the characters they
> see."[80]

Elements of the native system are painted on each frame of <u>Dance</u>

<u>Me Outside</u>. Meaning is derived from semiotic language and articulation

of codes painted with low key, realistic lighting, delineating Indian

characters in muted colors. The initial frames include a scintillating hint of

native noir, as natives emerge from the deep shadows, spewing evil,

threatening dialogue, setting the tone in parody of past genres. Close-up

frames relay intimate, action-reaction emotions which disclose

increasingly personal characteristics. Modern Indian wardrobe consisting

---

[59] Ibid, page 91.
[60] Ibid, page 85.

of denim, leather jackets, and flannel is coupled with indigenous body language and stylistic, richly woven, humorous inflection. Dialogue and trappings of material youth culture reflect universally similar career goals, relationship choices, and the desire for fast cars. The trickster's surreal longhouse, a crumbling brick building, represents the decay of colonial influence. The tone suggests a blend of "Indigenous West Side Story" and "Mad Max Comes to the Rez", reflecting realistic content woven in elevated, stylized parody form.

Gender differences are portrayed with a native twist, where feminine values are consistently more altruistic than male actions. This journey begins in parody but though the process of conflict and resolution, deep underlying truths are revealed. The film's theme is shaped by ascending, woven elements of surprise, as characterizations unfold and revelations appear which illustrate personal attitudes, desires, and emotions of an Indian family. The action centers on several problems which focus on protagonist Silas and his sister Iliana. The question answered in this film is comically posed by Frank Fencepost who mimicks throughout the film, "What do women really want?"

Questions of Iliana's non-Indian husband's infertility are resolved as she engineers her pregnancy with her ex-Indian boyfriend, an action necessary to achieve survival of her 'family,' although not completely altruistically. Ensuing characterizations reveal a romantic triangle, a murder, and the rules which define intertribal politics, providing a thought provoking view of an imperfect Indian reservation society.

The entertaining aspects of <u>Dance Me Outside</u>(*1994)* are especially explicit. Humorous elements reveal the "intertexuality evident between two texts, requiring that language have two simultaneous signifieds requiring reference."[61] This interpretation provides the ambiguity relevant to comedic signification, an extension of possibilities and meaning. Although native actors define the fundamental characterization and tone, interceding non-Indian elements intertextualize the gaze, adding a variety of alternative meanings which are not completely realistic but once again comic.

The process defines the distance between "horizon, knowledge, and commonality," between utterance and spectator, used to put him in touch with a world unknown to him through "context, contact, and code,"[62] in which he can construct models of self and difference. In this film, native

[61] Bahktin, Mikhail,& Cahtman, Seymour, Story and Discourse, Narrative Structure in Fiction and Film, page 167.
[62] Bahktin, Mikhail & Steiger, Janet, Interpreting Film, page 125.

women embody models of integrity and strength, setting the underlying rhythm of the film. Medicine woman Mad Etta reflects the paradoxical spiritual nature of the culture, as she dispenses wisdom and healing with her smoothie shake concoctions. Her ambiguity projects mixed auras of mystery, danger or insight, her meaning signals a good 'bru-ha' in this film. Silas's girlfriend Sadie is the epitome of justice and balance, whose actions benefit the community. Her image, shaped with soft angles and colors, signifies an angel of justice who has moral strength beyond her male counterpart or idealistic opponent, power which she wields with feministic altruism. Her mythic figure symbolizes success as well as morality and balance, acting as a bridge between conflicting ideologies.

Bizarre, extremely oppositional shadows are created by evil antagonists whose filmic codes consist of comedic colors, skinhead trappings and violent, anachronistic behavior and dialogue. The power of the skinheads is reflected in their deadly mortality, metaphoric representations of the colonial world. Their images embody a modern, extremely warped, punked out male version, the 'other' an icon of the patriarchal, antagonistic Federal Bureau of Investigation, who continually pose threats to the nature of native life. The skinheads are shot from a variety of extremely warped, hand held camera angles. Their extreme characterizations include primitive slang language, shaved heads, torn clothing and abusive, obnoxious actions. They display in your face confrontation and die violently, epitomizing internal and external imbalance.

Indigenous male characters manifest defensive positions in an effort to counter the violence, anarchy and greed projected by evil non-Indian male characters. Gooch, who is labeled 'jailbird' after serving a prison rap for selfdefense, sheds embodiments of 'either a killer or a Christian', neither of which are needed on the reservation. Objects and people acquire cultural identity through personal contact. The coyote trickster commandeers his brother-inlaw's sleek vehicle, adorning it with the trappings of an 'Indian Car', reflected later in a song of the same name. Following it's transformation, the car appears decorated with stickers, jacked up bumpers, feathers, and spewing rock music, a metaphoric image foreshadowing the brother-in-law's future as superficially adorned clan member. His external transformation is performed as a doubly reductive naming ceremony, designed to mask the real intent. But when his internal transformation takes place, he is accepted in a crucial moment by his Indian family. He loses trappings of the non-Indian world in an indigenized moment, but ultimately it is his underlying commitment to justice as an attorney which lends moral value, an explicit element underlying cross-cultural relations. In this film the non-Indian attorney becomes a fetishized cross-cultural urban construction, deconstructed in his rural form. The trickster characters, Silas and Frank Fencepost, contribute elements of humor and irony, indigenous metaphors designed to mythologize and define native worldview in a comical way.

The definitive element in <u>Dance Me Outside</u> which best articulates the native point of view, is the ideologic message symbolized by feminine power. Modern 'magic' is objectified and parodied in representations of healthy, smoothie drinking, psycho-therapeutic, proactive Indian women whose actions bond family and community. It is the women, Silas' mother, his sister Illiana and girlfiend Sadie who represent the glue holding the Indian community together. In this film Indian men simplistically externalize angry, violent male emotions, reflected from patriarchal males whose characters are over the top, out of control. Iliana's exceptional non-Indian husband, simplistically epitomized the thread of justice projected from that world. The Indian women are painted in natural style with non-voyeuristic camera angles and natural lighting, highlighting the essence of their beings as guardians of wisdom and power.

The solution to the question posed by John Smith in <u>Pocahontas:</u>

"What could be different about this new world?," is similar in these films. **In <u>Dance Me Outside,</u> the question: "What do women want?" is voiced throughout the narrative by native actor Adam Beach. Solutions appear as definitions of feminine character. Indian women represent the powerful ability to create just resolutions at sites of cultural conflict. They are the glue which nurtures, beautifies, and bonds elements of justice and truth, in a political and a cultural sense.**

Although the thematic question comically posed throughout the film by Frank was repetitive and frequently out of context, the answer also represents the collective Native American perspective since contact: **justice.** The solution is derived after the main characters resolve narrational obstructions which include: a murder, infertility, imprisonment, issues surrounding cross cultural marriage, the injustice of the U.S. legal system, career choices, the gang and drug culture, and poverty, all which bar them from establishing a contented family situation and a thriving community. (now we face gang, drug and organized crime infiltration, 2019)

Evolving representations of native centered cinema are reflected in all genres. Mikhail Bakhtin's "post-structuralist model of communication theory, translinguistical exchange, illustrates the exclusionary effects of language"[63] designed to set limits and personalize exchange. In <u>Dance Me Outside</u>, when conversation between mother and daughter turns to the subject of her non-Indian husband's infertility, the moment becomes a blatant, deeply personal linguistic utterance between intimate confidants. Language codes are also used to indigenize an extremely sensitive moment between ex-boyfriend Gooch (labeled as victim) and Illiana, in a conversation which defines complex underlying boundaries to her non-Indian husband. Camera angle and length of gaze relay impending doom, coupled with progressively shortened cuts, shifting angles, and extreme close-ups where dramatic emotional music paints another questionable voice in noir style.

The 'screen' which filters the tone of this film is represented in the first frames by Silas's interaction with a raven, the mythical trickster, a metaphoric mirror of himself, who bites his hand and takes his cigarette. Trickster characterization is described by writer Simon Ortiz as "a character which is changeable, interchangeable; he is shrewd but also a kind of fool at times." [64] He is one who lives and negotiates his life with

<hr>

[63] <u>Steirger, Janet, Interpreting Film</u>, page 120.
[64] Ortiz, Simon, <u>Winged Words</u>, page 106.

70

wit and style, outmaneuvering his enemies with a combination of realistic and mythic power, the native superman.

The demystified battles are enacted in tribal court, a reservation bar, during a parodied, doubly commodified sacred ceremony, and at the kitchen dinner table within a tribal community seeking justice. The film treatment reflects a visually realistic, emotionally empathic mixture of parody and somewhat realistic native identity. Entwined in noir structure, the story ends with a modern, feminized twist.

Definitive elements underlying new messages from Native America, compliment realistic cinematic conventions, integrating personal and political ideals with new form. The current debate in film semiotics is evident in different genres. Filmic devices employed now allow individuals to perceive with their eyes beyond timeless political constructions. But the crucial point of transformation will be seen in the ontological effects. The primary native elements in Indian film images now defines underlying questions of subjective and objective identity. As Indian writers now "come to the forefront, we will see more contemporary native characters emulating realistic life, who maintain their humor and sadness at the same time."[65] New native imagery now embodies subjective humor, irony, and empathic appeal. Using reflexive journeys of self-discovery packaged as 'a cultural product', poetically shaping elements, native writers are directing, producing, and financing their own artistic visions which paint natives as modern, mature individuals.

Dance Me Outside displays somewhat realistic dialogue and acting, mimicking the shift in audience demand for empathic, intelligent native subjects. Unfortunately the film lacks a true native core, highlighting the slapstick humor seen in stereotypic native representations. But Canadian native film representations have included the native soap opera format for several years as a precursor to the television series in which the,

> "spectator/mother identifies with each character in turn, is made to see 'the larger picture', affirming the primacy of the family by not showing an ideal family but one in turmoil."[66]

The film does reflect the growing demand for realistic native images resulting from shifting U.S. and Canadian demographics. Dance Me Outside, was produced by the Canadian Film Board which funds indigenous artists at a rate of five to our one American counterpart.

[65] Smith, Michael, President, American Indian Film Festival, San Francisco, 1997.
[66] Modeleski, Tania, Loving With a Vengeance, page 93.

Unfortunately, the film's budget outweighed sentiments for native direction.

One factor adding to expanded commercial explorations in independent native filmmaking are the coalitions formed between the Canadian Native Arts Council, the independent film community and U.S. Indian Communications Corporations.[67] Shifting demographics combined with renewed social vision, has spurned the creation of international native centered feature film projects. "If by art film it is meant, one dealing with an unusual theme in a non-conventional and frank manner, this picture fits this description aptly."[88] Evolving parallels are similar to postwar U.S. in June 1947, when the U.S. invasion of the French 'art' film influence began. Who was going to see these films? "Socially conscious patrons, groups who are tired of Hollywood fare and 'crave the stronger realism of the better grade imported film.'"[88] According to Gallup Poll figures the patrons of these art house moviegoers were , "GI's just returned from Europe, people in higher socio-economic brackets, the better educated." [68] Consumer markets were grouped by 'class cultures', and became engaged with "selling symbols as well as merchandise." U.S. audiences were drawn

---

[67] Farmer, Gary, Editor in Chief, Aboriginal Voices, Interview, 1998. [88] Straiger, Janet, Interpreting Film, page 182-3.
[68] Ibid, page 189.

to art films containing "realistic treatment, dramatic acting, socially significant messages and improbable happenings."[90]   The patrons of art films were typified as intellectuals or more likely as 'eggheads'. The tone of the film was valued over the content, adding to the realistic, personalized filmic nature which also illustrates the tone of contemporary native art films produced today.

When natives began to participate in unmasking the rhetorical, by employing definitive semiotic devices of our own, defining our cultural history, did views about us change. Now that we are actively participating in construction of our realistic cinematic aesthetic, new multicultural standards are emerging in independent Indian film imagery. New versions encompass a mix of voices and include the histories of marginalized groups, reflecting our public and private spirits. In these films, native and non-native characters are unmasked, revealing secrets and information which undoubtedly influences our collective behavior.

---

[91] Straiger, Janet, <u>Interpreting Film</u>, page 187.

SMOKE SIGNALS (1997)

The idealistic message in <u>Smoke Signals,</u> underlies the "overpowering realism with a passionate sense of human fortitude" seen in 'art' films. Relaying the idealism and irony seen in contemporary Indian life, the film was shaped by the hands of an experienced native director who imaginatively interpreted the discourse of a Native American writer. This interpretation is pure genius.

Sherman Alexi and Chris Eyre's film adaptation of Alexi's short story, <u>This is what it Means to Say Pheonix, Arizona,</u> resulted in the Sundance Film Festival's 1997 audience award winning film <u>Smoke Signals</u> (1997). It is the first independently produced US based film employing native discourse, direction, and talent, which has also found relative commercial success. Alexi and Eyre meld technical ability and native cultural style, resulting in a realistic, entertaining collaboration which textures indigenous identity into an art film about death and rebirth. By employing filmic conventions used to express personalized, dreamlike messages within the filmic dream, a personal secret is revealed which is again, a metaphor for generations of native alienation and unrest. Ironic social commentary is used to color this adventure, in shaping dramatic characterizations of native life.

Now that Indian directors, writers, and actors are emerging to re-engineer our self-imagery, historic gaps are filled with personal perspectives on the big screen. Chris Eyre, Arapaho director of <u>Smoke Signals</u> *(1997)*, combines his native sensibility with filmic technique. His experience with filmmaking allows him to counterbalance the ideologic effects which have influenced acceptance of natives where, "Hollywood uses the Indian as a vehicle. There is a lot of subtext involved compared with putting a white person on the screen."[69]

Upon receiving several degrees in film making, Chris Eyre determined to re-engineer cinematic images of Indians by taking an objective, realistic approach to directing because,

> "the only way we have been portrayed is by non-Indians, so it is a rebirth. In terms of trying to portray Indians in a good light, what it comes down to is trusting us as Indian writers, directors, and producers."[70]

Director Chris Eyre, as well as other native artists are inscribing new information in definitive auteur style upon American culture. The current cinematic trend in native filmmaking reflects the ability of the auteur

---

[69] Eyre, Chris, Telephone Interview, 1998.
[70] Ibid, 1998.

filmmaker to subjectively contextualize signifier and transformation, seeking an *inner consistency* with theme, structure, and style, "which makes an interpretation relevant, connecting film to semantic fields which interest people generally." [94]

Native authorial voice now reflects practical perspective in a world where inequality is still prevalent. Signification of the Indian experience, "is used to communicate known truths and the aesthetic function of questioning, expanding itself as a code"[95]   In Smoke Signals, Thomas Builds-the-Fire consistently mocks protagonist Victor's subconscious thoughts whining,   "What about your Dad? Why did he leave? Didn't he love you?" begging an answer to the ugly question, the answer entwined with the natural beauty of the aesthetic.

Native inflection is mimicked by the use of *objects*, where personalized things become powerful allies in poetically parodied signification. In this film, fire simulates meaningful, powerful representations of evil and death, which evolve into imagery signifying rebirth and forgiveness. Frybread acquires mythical power, extending feminine strength to iconic, Jesus-like proportions, countering the devastating effects of genocide, alienation, and

[95] Bordwell, David, Making Meaning, page 105.
[94] Bordwell, David, Making Meaning, page 127.

alcoholism plaguing generations of Native Americans. In the naturalization process of authorship, native history is relayed through a timeline of conquorers. Memories reconstruct the devastating effects of Columbus, Christ, the Jesuits, and egotistical Custer, with dialogue lending cynical predictions of future Indian holocausts at the hands of alternate invaders.

The basketball court becomes iconic battleground for modern war games where, "The Indian warriors won against the Jesuits for one day," reflecting native people's continual conflict with annihilistic, patriarchal religious ideals. The media becomes the representative voice of the Reservation, portrayed by radio script layered with indigenized slang and inflection, "Ho-la! Look at that cloud." Rush hour traffic information is so slow that it turns to meditative reflection and personalized commentary, reduced to gossip.

Aerial shots define boundaries and landscape of the Cour D'Alene Indian Reservation. Additionally, the new native aesthetic works "within the tradition, or genre of films from which it comes," [71] providing localized information to the generic, coming of age, road trip structure. New

---

[71] Andrew, Dudley, <u>Film Theory,</u> page 109.

personalities constructed as part of the aesthetic, are now three-dimensional characters who reveal underlying elements of the culture.

Thomas Builds-the-Fire becomes protagonist Victor's sensitized subconscious and alter ego. His character embodies an intellectual, annoying, slightly clairvoyant nerd who acts as catalyst of memory and originator of new illusions and dreams. In the initial frames of the film, Victor's father Arnold dies a spiritual death surrounded by flames and travels through the remainder 'vanishing,' touching people with his 'magic'. Perpetuated by alcohol and delusion, he attempts to reunite body and soul. Author Alexi is seen graveside in a fleeting few frames at the end of the film in a personalized statement, his anthem of self-realization. Alexi's message speaks to and for a large proportion of Native America, whose subconscious journeys of self-discovery initiate public and private reconstructions.

Eyre's sensitized camera eye fashions beautifully descriptive, expressive impressions of contemporary Native America. His narrative style characterizes the modern native buddy theme, woven on a road trip structure which embodies existentialist detail, transcends ambiguous feelings and recreates transformative moments. The meta-narration inscribes metaphors laden 'heavy with illusions,' which reflect another essential message of the Native American experience since colonial contact. In viewing the film, the audience unlocks the underlying codes of illusion through experiential identity formation, mimicked in indigenized language code. Ambiguous relational models of native identity are replaced with uncovered truths. Throughout the journey the effects of genocide are bared, revealing heightened levels and effects of alcoholism, poverty, and cultural annihilation.

The road trip structure takes Victor and Thomas on a journey through canyons and country, on a bus heavily laden with modernized, cowboy-Indian and gender conflict. They pose and answer the question in parody, "Why don't you ever see John Wayne's teeth, Hey-ya?" satirizing historical illusion. Articulated in repetitive native narrative set to music, it is one of several songs written by author Sherman Alexi. Although the issues are artistically portrayed, the filmic seams are still apparent.

Most importantly, the artistic agendas of Native Americans now embody structural myths and rituals of the subconscious. In <u>Smoke Signals,</u> the audience is taken on the protagonists' journey, redefining memory with projected dream imagery. The shaping of dream images allows us to intimate and, "mimick exchanges between body and a material world, allowing us to see through reflections and pose questions about the technological, psychological, and sociological processes."[72]

In the film, secrets are revealed within a reservation community which create suffering but also strengthen deep underlying bonds of love and forgiveness. The physical journey begins the healing process, which acts as a catalyst for family and community. Truth is a transformative tool and becomes a metaphoric representation of desire for the collective native experience since contact, replacing iconic Christian ideals. Protagonist Victor attempts to be true to modern native culture but he is caught between racial stereotypes and personal conflict, initializing his journey of self-realization and recovery. The film's theme weaves roots of the native tradition with aspects of patriarchy, family dynamics, faith, forgiveness, and healing.

It is the realistic trend in native film representation, which delivers a new "pre-structuralist source,"[73] relaying social message from author to audience, creating thought provoking narrative forms by pairing story and storyteller. In <u>Smoke Signals</u>, authorial voice and camera eye have deep

---

[72] Andrew, Dudley, <u>Film Theory</u>, page 35.
[73] Ibid, page 146.

roots in native tradition, "replacing the representations of cosmic and religious space"[74] by answering the question, "What does it mean to be an Indian?" In this version of a young Indian man's life, the payoffs are psychological, social, and entertaining. The narrative weaves social commentary with ironic parody. The collective thread which runs throughout the film is once again, the power of justice, truth, and beauty personified by women who counterbalance the aggressive, malicious ideals underlying social injustice.

Now we can show ways in which our culture negotiates the dominant system, emphasize key points, and paradoxically expand from there with indigenized eye. The new conversation takes place on Indian turf, where social and cultural context evokes deeply empathic moments as well as cynical, ironic humor. Native and non-native characters are unmasked, revealing secrets and personal information. In native film culture, 'unity of action' reflects the ability of the artist to poetically combine elements of oral storytelling, tribal histories, and unique humor within a modern framework, supporting the worldview of native people.

In a subjectively surreal approach, Eyre shapes the native characters of

---

[74] Arnheim, Rudolf, Film Art, page 23.

Victor and Thomas by allowing the narrative to connect in a series of 'dreams'

and memories which occur as flashbacks. Identity is painted with a combination of mythical belief, surreal illusions, and realistic detail. Visions of the real become realistic visions. The objectification of native worldview illustrates nuance of the dominant culture, reflected by natives.

Irony and cynicism play a large part in painting Indian character in this film, which is sad and sometimes trite. Characterizations of Thomas Buildsthe-Fire and his grandmother relay particular sensitivity with intelligent humor. Dressed in paradoxical non-Indian nerd fashion, Thomas loses and regains the external trappings of white society in his narrative trajectory. The indigenized camera lens allows the eye to "filter and enlarge perception through a 'cultural screen', allowing perceptual deviation and conferring of value, making a representation significant"[75] Reflecting the conflicts and frustration of identity formation plaguing Native America, Victor demands that Thomas become a 'real Indian' by taking off his suit, take on a sullen, stoic expression, and being cynical.

But Victor's forgiving, sensitive nature remains consistently true to character, reflected in his love for his grandmother, his ability to forgive

---

[75] Andrew, Dudley, Film Theory, page 20.

and live in the present. His re-envisioned memories provide solutions, filling gaps with subconscious, partially fictive constructs. Victor's character embodies the subconscious journey which many Native Americans have taken as they lose collective baggage and dysfunction, the generational effects of genocide. The new native aesthetic is a product of socially conscientious, subjectively entertaining 'objective realism'. Hollywood is said to have created new versions of native identity each few years, but the new characterizations seen in <u>Smoke Signals</u> (1997) present a different perspective of life on the 'Rez,'. New complex Native American identity adds another layer to the native aesthetic as a serious art form.

Although Indian cinema has been a work in progress, the new journey is visually riveting and empathetically real. New characterizations traverse untouched emotional ground in dramatic recreations of modernized native rituals of exchange. The new commercial explorations legitimize the psychological, social, and artistic payoffs while highlighting native actors, who engage a mixture of languages, traditional and modern beliefs, based in signification of rural and urban Indian experience.

The result is an expression of spiritual and artistic identity which opens minds and hearts. The perspective encompasses the views of people who reflect cultural, spiritual, and traditional ideals. The new native aesthetic is defined by native artists who establish key issues and strive to prove the unproven about the culture, using a range of emotions and objects which stimulate associations. This is a different version of commercial exploration, unmasking native and non-native characters, occasionally using the culture of violence to get to issues.

Native American artists in the 1990's are attempting to create their representations with historical accuracy and creativity. A large part of the characterization of the native culture is entwined in defending our right to sovereignty and in breaking predetermined stereotypical patterns. Native American cinema may be experiencing a revolutionary period based on expanded technical expertise and the readiness of gaming tribes, who may provide an economic window of opportunity for image creation and interpretation. For Indians, the funding opportunities may open a wider range of realistic, uncensored imagery in all genres. Screenwriter Randy Tinkerman believes, "This is the beginning of an explosion of new native imagery seen in commercial genres."[76]

Renewed rituals of exchange modernized in neo-native forms, "Have

---

[76] Tinkerman, Randall, Screenwriter, Hiawatha, 1998.

allowed people to connect between communities as they did 100 years ago."[77] As we explore new territory and recreate our histories, using tools that capture moments of inspiration, we share in creating new identity and transformational forms of reality, told with dreams and stories. Information and insight delivers greater fulfillment to us all.

The Indian community is experiencing re-emerging oral history and community strength. People are networking, sharing ideas and dreams, reappearing in new versions of traditional, modernized identity in pursuit of collective voice. The effects of technology reflect the heightened pace with which we are connecting between groups, largely shaped by a new generation of Indians who travel between rural and urban worlds, creating new geographical sites of authorship. They may represent the emerging spirit of Native America and define their own historical mission. Native youth want to participate in actively building their contemporary world, melding traditional culture with modern technology, not support and emulate Barbie doll imagery, [78] which will continue the cyclical identification that binds and "perpetuates negative images, at the same time attempting to transcend stereotypes."[79]

---

[77] Personal Interview, American Indian Film Festival, 1997.
[78] Lac Courte Oreilles Focus Group, 1997.
[79] Rollins, Peter, Film and History, The Hollywood Indian, page 5.

The creative messages which native storytellers and artists express is one of wholeness and survival, evolving from the way in which we live, characteristics embodied by storyteller artistry and the rhetoric of diversity. Despite the continued protests from within the culture, specific symbolic messages with political significance are inherently perpetuated in images of Native America. Although new images now being shaped by Native American hands are creating a visual dialogue between cultures.

At the heart of those raised in the Indian culture, is the ability to maintain structural myths and rituals of the subconscious which define Native America. Those who seek to find their soul, and in the process the soul of humanity, define the 'other' among people unlike themselves, which may explain the continual fascination with indigenous people who have managed to maintain aspects of their cultural and spiritual identity. At the heart of the Native American culture is possession of histories, myths, and contemporary culture. It is the artistic agenda of Indians which defies stereotype, is beyond representation because it exists through place, culture, and vision, with shadows of memory lost. Attempting to find those moments creates many enlightening possibilites.

Self Reflexive Native American Film

One of the most remarkable things about the emerging Indian filmic genre is to see how narrowly it resembles the static stereotype of indigenous communities. New Native American cinematic images present characters whose lives are complex and emotional. They occupy a sense of place, time, and unity. Issues of cultural identity, in addition to political voice enter artistic agendas. New times are calling for new images, free of twodimensional and derogatory native characters popularized by non-native ideologies. Does the new aesthetic reflect an emergence of Native American economic power, is this new genre provoked by spectator desire, or a push from within the culture to create realistic forms? The answer is a reflection of time and place.

The effects of the emerging Native American filmic genre can be seen by the emotional impact it makes on the audience, showing us that each generation must take responsibility for shaping it's representations. Although social contracts are born, stylized, and evolve daily, it is individuals and their respective cultures who must either accept the effects of representations, or create reflexive forms. As consumers we either impose the rules (upon ourselves) or accept them in economic exchange. Indians can now hope to create entertainment value while remaining true to our culture, by linking identity to real personalities who are rooted in our cultural heritage, affecting positive change with contact.

Bibliography

Andrew, Dudley, <u>Concepts in Film Theory,</u> Oxford University Press, 1984.

Arnheim, Rudolf<u>, Film as Art,</u>University of California Press, 1957.

Austin, Bruce A., Editor, <u>Current Research in Film: Audiences, Economics, and Law,</u> Ablex Publishing Corporation, 1987.

Barthes, Roland, <u>The Pleasure of the Text,</u> The Noonday Press, 1975.

Barthes, Roland, <u>Camera Lucida, Reflections on Photography,</u> The

Noonday Press, 1981.

Bataille, Gretchen M. and Silet, Charles L., <u>The Pretend Indians, Images of</u>
<u>Native Americans in the Movies,</u> The Iowa State University Press, 1980.

Bordwell, David, <u>Making Meaning: Inference and Rhetoric in the Interpretation of Cinema,</u> Harvard University Press, 1989.

Berger, John, <u>Ways of Seeing,</u> Penguin Books Ltd., 1977.

Berkhofer,Robert F. Jr, <u>The White Man's Indian, Images of the American Indians from Columbus to the Present, First Vintage Books, 1979.</u>

Chatman, Seymour<u>, Story and Discourse, Narrative Structure in Fiction</u> and <u>Film,</u> Cornell University Press, 1986.

Coltelli, Laura, <u>Winged Words</u>, <u>American Indian Writers Speak,</u> University of   Nebraska Press, 1990.

Curtis, Edward S., <u>Prayer to the Great Mystery, The Uncollected Writings</u> and <u>Photography of Edward S. Curtis, 1995.</u>

Mast, Gerald, <u>A Short History of the Movies</u>, University of Chicago, 1986.

Rollins, Peter, The Hollywood Indian, University of Miami, 1993.

Staiger, Janet, Interpreting Film, Princeton University Press, 1992.

Steadman, Raymond William, Shadows of the Indian, Stereotypes in American   Culture, University of Oklahoma Press: Norman, 1982.

Vizenor, Gerald, Manifest Manners: Postindian Warriors of Survivance, Wesleyan   University Press, 1994.

Vizenor, Gerald, Native Amerian Literature, A Brief Introduction and Anthology, Harper Collins College Publishers, 1995.

Vizenor, Gerald, Narrative Chance, Postmodern Discourse on Native American Indian Literatures, University of Oklahoma Press, 1993.

Journals

Taguma, Lori J., Native Americans in Cinema History, Sundance Film Festival Catalogue, 1998: 91.

Hill, Richard, Why I Hate Star Trek, The Hollywood Indian is Alive and Well and Living in Outer Space, Aboriginal Voices Magazine, March 1998: 43.

Taguma, Lori J., Smoke Signals - All Native Film Has Fresh Perspective, Aboriginal Voices, March 1998: 41.

Filmography

American Scene, Director Dan Jones, 1997.

Billy Jack, Director Tom Laughlin, 1971.

Dance Me Outside, Director Brian Dennis, 1994.

Dances With Wolves, Director Kevin Costner, 1994.

Grand Avenue, Director Greg Sarris, HBO, 1996.

House Made of Dawn, Director Richardson Morse, 1972.

In the Land of the War Canoes: Kwakiutl Indian Life on the Northwest Coast, Director Edward S. Curtis,1914.

Lakota Woman, Director Hanay Geiogamah, HBO, 1994 .

Naturally Native, Director Valerie Redhorse, The Mashantucket Pequot Tribe, 1997.

Powwow Highway, Director Jonathan Wacks, 1989.

Pocahontas, Disney Corporation, 1994.

Silent Tears, Director Shirley Cheechoo, Canadian Film Board, 1997.

Smoke Signals, Director Chris Eyre, Miramax, 1997.

The Lone Ranger, Director Clayton Moore, 1947.

The Searchers, Director John Ford, 1956.

The Shadow Catcher: Edward S. Curtis and the North American Indian, Director T.C. McLuhan & Edward S. Curtis, 1974 .

Thunderheart, Director Michael Apted, 1992.

Walks Far Woman, Director , 1983.

Interviews

Alexi, Sherman. Personal interview. Author, <u>Smoke Signals.</u> Sundance Film Festival, 20 January 1998.

Blythe, Frank. Personal interview. American Indian Film Finance Consortium, San Francisco, 10 November, 1997.

Eyre, Chris. Telephone interview. Director, <u>Smoke Signals.</u> 15 November 1997.

Dettloff, Robert. Personal interview. Animator, Disney Corporation, Los Angeles, CA.   20 December 1997.

Dutton, Michael E. Personal interview. Director, Public Relations, Mashantucket Pequot Tribal Nation. American Indian Film Finance Seminar, San Francisco, CA, 10 November, 1997.

Farmer, Gary. Personal interview. Editor<u>, Aboriginal Voices</u>, Toronto, Canada. Sundance Film Festival, 10 March, 1998.

Lac Courte Oreilles Tribe. Cultural Renewal Focus Groups. Lac Courte Oreilles, Hayward, Wisconsin. 25 August 1997.

Sarris, Greg. Telephone interview. 20 January, 1998.

Smith, Michael. Personal interview. American Indian Film Festival, 10 November 1997.

Tinkerman, Randall. Hiawatha Screenwriter, American Indian Film Finance Seminar,   San Francisco, 10 November, 1997.

Lecture

Bourdeau, Pierre. Address. Lecture. University of California, Berkeley. Berkeley, CA.   20 March, 1996.

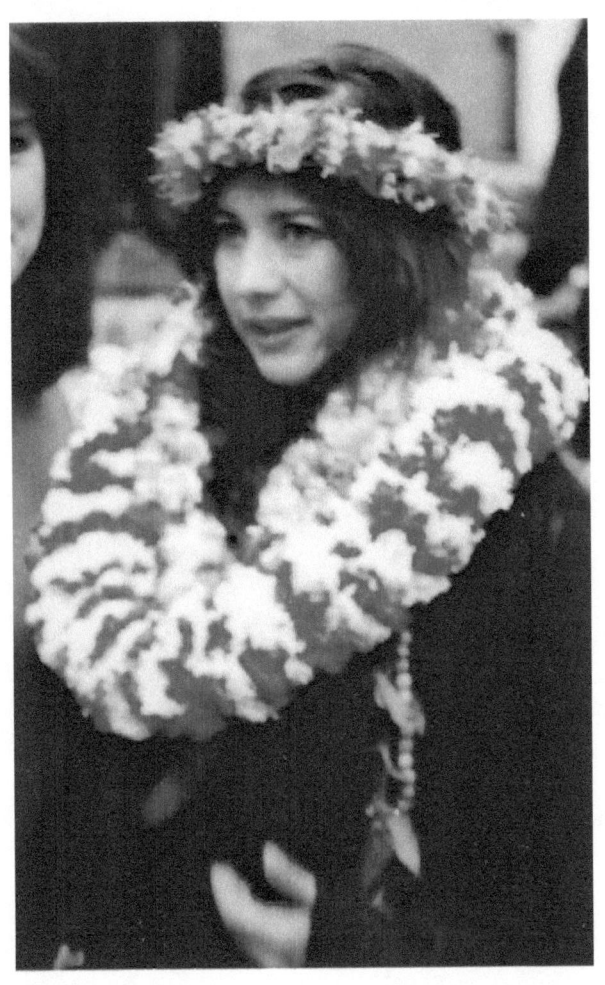

Lori J. Taguma, University of California Berkeley, 1999.